THE ZODIAC GUIDE TO
LEO

ASTRID CARVEL

This edition first published in 2024 by Red Wheel, an imprint of
Red Wheel/Weiser, LLC
With offices at:
65 Parker Street, Suite 7
Newburyport, MA 01950
www.redwheelweiser.com

ISBN: 978-1-59003-545-0

Printed and bound in China
1010 Printing International Ltd
10 9 8 7 6 5 4 3 2 1

Contents

4   INTRODUCTION

6   PART 1
     WELCOME TO THE ZODIAC

34   PART 2
     MEET LEO

62   PART 3
     YOUR HOROSCOPE AND YOU

98   PART 4
     ASTROLOGY FOR SELF-CARE

124 FAREWELL

125 RESOURCES

Introduction

Are you ready to open your mind to the ancient wisdom of the zodiac and explore the possibilities contained within? Astrology is as far-reaching as the night sky itself, an intricate web of stars, constellations, planets, celestial spheres and horizons, mapped out by ancient cultures in millennia gone by in an attempt to make sense of our time on Earth.

This book will equip you with the tools you need to explore more deeply your behaviors, characteristics and connections; to open up the possibilities held in the movement of the planets, and help you to find guidance and comfort when you need it.

Astrology is a voyage of self-discovery, into which you can dip or dive as you wish, taking on a few morsels from the stars or getting stuck in to the complexities held within.

Among these pages you'll find a wealth of insight into the history of the zodiac and the different astrological traditions. You'll learn how to build your own birth chart, what it all means and what you can gain from it.

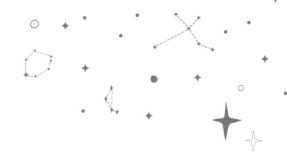

You'll look at how the position of the planets contain meaning, how to decipher your sun, moon and rising signs, and more. You'll look at the houses – the segments of the sky that relate to different aspects of your life – and how to decode their teachings. The patterns created by celestial matter across the houses are decoded here in order for you to easily digest what it all means.

Then you'll move on to the details of your sun sign and how it relates to all areas of your existence, as well as the self-care practices you can benefit from, with ideas and suggestions specific to your sign of the zodiac.

So, what are you waiting for? Turn the page and let the journey begin.

Part 1

WELCOME TO THE ZODIAC

This chapter will take you on a journey through the birth of the zodiac, thousands of years ago, to its relevance in modern times. To understand your sun sign – often referred to as your zodiac or star sign – you might first want to delve into the history and traditions that led to the widely practiced movement that is known today. What moved people to look to the sky for guidance long ago and why do people still do it? Research suggests that today astrology is more popular than ever. It has experienced something of a resurgence, perhaps because the myriad uncertainties of life push people towards the darkness above in search of comfort. The far-reaching knowledge of the stars is yours for the taking – are you ready?

What is astrology?

Before you go any further, it's important to differentiate between astronomy and astrology. **Astronomy** is the scientific study of the universe, including planets, stars, celestial objects and space itself. **Astrology** looks at how the position of the stars and planets at the time of our birth can affect our personality and shape how we live our lives.

While astrology is an interpretation of the position of the planets and stars, it relates closely to human behavior and the influence of celestial bodies on our everyday choices, moods and behavior. Astrologers believe that everything is part of an interconnected reality and that understanding how the ancient symbolism of the stars and planets can relate to events in your own life is a constantly evolving process.

While astrology does not suppose that the planets and stars control you, nor does it predict the future, it does suggest that the celestial sphere is able to create certain conditions and situations that you can learn to use to your advantage. It might take practice, but the potential in the stars is there for the taking.

Horoscopes in magazines and newspapers are just the tip of the iceberg. To find out what makes you tick from an astrological perspective you simply need to know your birth date. From there you can uncover your sun, moon and rising signs, create a birth chart and learn more about yourself. We'll get to those later. The world of astrology is far-reaching and open to all, and can help you to understand your foibles, behaviors and relationships. It can help you decode your past and open your mind to the future.

The first step on your celestial path is a crucial one – it's time to learn about the zodiac.

History of the zodiac

Long before people could travel into space – or even before telescopes allowed us to study worlds beyond ours in more detail – humans gazed up at the night sky to keep track of the time of year and planned their lives around the position of the stars. Many a traveller has looked to the sky to determine which route to take, with ancient sailors putting their trust in the celestial map and using the North Star for guidance. In ancient Egypt farmers were prewarned of the annual Nile flood in July by the rising of Sirius, the Dog Star. The Phoenicians assessed the Sun's position in the heavens when they needed to know which direction to take, and a lunar calendar led by the phases of the moon was drawn up by ancient cultures to keep track of religious events.

While it's something of a mystery when exactly the signs of the zodiac became linked to human characteristics and behaviors, we do know that they originated as a time-measuring device. By mapping out the constellations in a strip of the sky spanning the circumference of the Earth – in which the Sun, Moon and planets moved – and dividing that strip into 12 segments, early astrologers were able to create a calendar of zodiac signs.

The sky is divided into 12 segments and each is occupied by a zodiac sign. Each sign is represented by a constellation that loosely outlines the symbol attached to that sign, and it takes approximately one month for the Sun to travel through each sign's segment. This is the reason that in astrology the signs of the zodiac are known as Sun signs.

While the Ancient Greeks are largely thought to be responsible for devising the Zodiac calendar we are familiar with today, there is evidence of the Babylonians living by a similar set of signs as far back as 1500 BCE.

Why does the zodiac calendar start in March?

The Ancient Greeks believed the first day of spring occurred when the sun appeared in the constellation Aries, marking the beginning of the calendar. It made sense for the year to start with the green shoots emerging after winter, with spring signifying new beginnings.

How it works

There are myriad techniques and applications when it comes to astrology, but the most widely used in the West today is modern or psychological astrology (see page 28).

Before you do anything else, you need to create your birth chart. In the modern age, this can be done quite easily using the internet, however before the technological age those in search of answers in the stars had to search great reams of dusty pages to find the information they needed to compile their trusted chart.

Your birth chart maps out the position of the key stars and planets in the sky on the day you were born. This chart is the basis for every horoscope or reading you might have. An astrologer – or you once you get the hang of it – compares your birth chart with the position of the planets and stars at key moments to understand your motivations. Knowing how the planets behave allows for predictions about an individual's behavior to be gauged in certain situations and at a certain time. None of this is a given, but many find comfort in being granted an insight into their psyche.

Combining the planetary movements with information about your sun or zodiac sign, along with your moon and rising signs (see pages 76–81), as well as your element (see page 24) you can gather more information about what really makes you tick and even understand why certain characteristics of your personality differ from those of other people in your life.

Throughout this book you'll learn about the different aspects of astrology that allow you to access a clearer picture of yourself.

Useful terms

Zodiac – this is a band across the sky through which the Sun, Moon and visible planets move throughout the year. The zodiac is divided into 12 segments according to the constellations that represent the 12 sun signs – Aries, Taurus, Gemini, Cancer, Leo, Virgo, Libra, Scorpio, Sagittarius, Capricorn, Aquarius and Pisces.

Sun sign – this is your sign in the zodiac, relating to when you were born; for example, if you were born on 21 April your sun sign would be Taurus.

Birth chart – a birth chart is a snapshot of the position of the planets on the day you were born.

Planets – in astrology the planets refer to those in the solar system – Mercury, Venus, Mars, Jupiter, Saturn, Neptune and Pluto (despite this being declassified in more recent times). The Sun and Moon are also considered planets in modern astrology.

Houses – 12 segments of the night sky that overlap the signs of the zodiac. Each house reflects a different area of your life.

Elements – each sun sign is assigned one of four elements – fire, water, air or earth.

Moon sign – your moon sign is the sign of the zodiac where the Moon was positioned on the day of your birth.

Rising sign – your rising sign is the sign of the zodiac that was rising (or ascending) on the eastern horizon on the day of your birth.

Retrograde – this refers to an optical illusion that makes it look like the planets are moving backwards, due to their movement through the night sky relative to the Earth.

Midpoint – a midpoint is the measured halfway point between two celestial objects on your chart.

Horoscope – your horoscope is an astrological map of the positions of the Sun, Moon and planets at a given moment in time in relation to your sun, moon and rising signs. This map can be used to help understand past events or hint towards future ones.

Your sun sign

Sun signs are simply another way of referring to star or zodiac signs. With the Earth making one full revolution of the Sun per year, it spends around one month in each of the 12 zodiac signs. Your sun sign is determined by your birth date: whichever sign - be that Aries, Taurus, Gemini, Cancer, Leo, Virgo, Libra, Scorpio, Sagittarius, Capricorn, Aquarius or Pisces - the Sun was transiting through at the time you were born is that which is astrologically assigned to you.

It is impossible to be a "pure" Aries, for example, because all of the other planets would have to be positioned in your sign's segment of the sky at the time of your birth, which due to their orbits and distance from each other could never happen. With the Sun considered the most influential of the celestial objects in your horoscope, your sun sign is believed to be a valuable source from which to learn a great deal about yourself.

However, in order to gain a complete picture of yourself, you must analyse the Sun's influence alongside that of the other planets in your horoscope - the most important being your rising and moon signs. If you don't yet know your signs, you'll learn how to determine these on the following pages. These vital elements of your birth chart (see page 70) help to uncover cosmic insights into your character and inner workings.

How to calculate your sun sign

Working out your sun sign is simple. Check the list below for the sign that falls on your birthday.

Aries	–	21 March–20 April
Taurus	–	21 April–21 May
Gemini	–	22 May–21 June
Cancer	–	22 June–22 July
Leo	–	23 July–23 August
Virgo	–	24 August–22 September
Libra	–	23 September–23 October
Scorpio	–	24 October–22 November
Sagittarius	–	23 November–21 December
Capricorn	–	22 December–20 January
Aquarius	–	21 January–18 February
Pisces	–	19 February–20 March

The signs

ARIES *(21 March–20 April)*

Symbol: Ram
Element: Fire
Ruling planet: Mars

Aries people are brave and headstrong, but can also be childish, impatient and impulsive. They are determined and direct, able to be both straightforward and clear-headed when making decisions. Aries people are natural born leaders and, much like their animal counterpart the ram, they are fiercely independent. They are very passionate thrill-seekers with a zest for life.

TAURUS *(21 April–21 May)*

Symbol: Bull
Element: Earth
Ruling planet: Venus

Taurus people are patient and dependable, persevering to the very end. They show untold loyalty to family and friends, and their quiet strength and determination is an inspiration to others. A Taurus is not a fan of change and does not like being rushed. They long for stability and home comforts. In relationships, Tauruses look for emotional security – they may take their time looking for it, but when they find it, they work hard to hold on to it.

<u>GEMINI</u> *(22 May–21 June)*

Symbol: Twin
Element: Air
Ruling planet: Mercury

Geminis are cheerful and upbeat people, while also being curious and rational. They are good communicators and are incredibly sociable, often keen to engage with anyone and everyone they meet. A Gemini's twin element sees two sides to their personality, and they also have a fickle and superficial nature that they need to work to control. They seek a lively rapport in relationships and have a knack of finding something in common with everyone.

<u>CANCER</u> *(22 June–22 July)*

Symbol: Crab
Element: Water
Ruling planet: the Moon

Cancerians are caring souls who are immensely protective of their friends and loved ones. Much like that of their animal counterpart, the crab, they project a tough, shell-like exterior to conceal their sensitivity. Headstrong and stubborn, it can be difficult to convince a Cancerian to give something up when they have it in their sights. They can also be argumentative, but an overriding kindness runs deep with this sign.

LEO *(23 July–23 August)*

Symbol: Lion
Element: Fire
Ruling planet: the Sun

Leos are attention-seekers who bring energy to those around them. They love nothing more than to have an adoring audience and are proud of their flamboyance. A Leo excels in both creativity and organization, and can be quick to impress this on others whose lives are more chaotic – sometimes without invitation. Leos are often the more dominant in relationships, but bring kindness, warmth and generosity with them.

VIRGO *(24 August–22 September)*

Symbol: Maiden
Element: Earth
Ruling planet: Mercury

Virgos are constantly on the go, busier than all the other signs and in constant pursuit of perfection. Practical, organized and thoughtful people, Virgos are always willing to offer assistance or advice and will help whenever they can. While kind and patient in relationships, a Virgo can also require reassurance to boost their confidence and relax into their situation.

LIBRA *(23 September–23 October)*

Symbol: Scales
Element: Air
Ruling planet: Venus

Libras use their skills of diplomacy to strive for peace and harmony in all areas of their lives. When it comes to decision-making, they can ruminate at length and often seek the advice of others for guidance. These charming individuals tend to shy away from high-pressure situations in order to find a happier balance. A Libra is both romantic and generous when it comes to relationships, however they harbor high expectations in love.

SCORPIO *(24 October–22 November)*

Symbol: Scorpion
Element: Water
Ruling planet: Pluto

Scorpio is one of the more emotional signs of the zodiac, with jealousy an overriding theme that they work hard to contain. However, combined with strong willpower, this can often drive them to reach for their goals. With boundless energy, Scorpios are often high achievers, and their knack for deep, analytical thought pushes them to get to the root of problems. In relationships, when a Scorpio sets their sights on someone, they do all they can to get what they want – and are fiercely loyal.

SAGITTARIUS *(23 November–21 December)*

Symbol: Archer
Element: Fire
Ruling planet: Jupiter

Sagittarians are thrill-seekers who are always up for a challenge and in pursuit of adventure. Their enthusiasm and optimism can be infectious, leading them to be popular among others who often enjoy their company and zest for life. In relationships, Sagittarians don't like to be restricted, and their independent spirit and rest-lessness can lead them to grow bored easily, needing romantic situations to remain fresh and exciting.

CAPRICORN *(22 December–20 January)*

Symbol: Goat
Element: Earth
Ruling planet: Saturn

Capricorns are realistic and carefully approach situations in a logical manner. Slow and steady wins the race with this sign – with Capricorns quietly moving towards the prize with composure and without haste. A unique sense of humor is a key trait of a Capricorn and, when it comes to relationships, they are both loyal and devoted.

AQUARIUS *(21 January–18 February)*

Symbol: Water-bearer
Element: Air
Ruling planet: Uranus

Aquarians are often glamourous, eccentric people, always friendly and often overly helpful. They are genuinely curious about everyone they meet and will quiz them at great length about their lives, however they tend to shroud their own in mystery. In relationships Aquarians are independent and need their space, which can make it hard to settle down.

PISCES *(19 February–20 March)*

Symbol: Fish
Element: Water
Ruling planet: Neptune

Pisceans are kind people, often going out of their way to be both friendly and charitable. This gentle sign promotes compassion and understanding, and a Pisces is not afraid to wear their heart on their sleeve – opening up and sharing their feelings with those they care for. In relationships Pisceans can be overly affectionate and often keep their emotions close to the surface.

The elements

The 12 sun signs are split into four groups, with each represented by an element. Traditionalists believe these vital elements make up the entire universe. Fire, air, water and earth are regarded as the four basic principles of life, in turn corresponding to four basic principles of the psyche. Knowing our element sign allows us to probe further into the characteristics associated with it.

FIRE

Fire signs: Aries, Leo, Sagittarius

Fire signs are bright and sparky, artistic and passionate. You can expect them to be confident in their independence and never afraid to speak up. Ever the optimists, fire signs make things happen and don't mind the pressure that might come along with it.

AIR

Air signs: Libra, Aquarius, Gemini

Air signs are social creatures, they know how to work the room and offer engaging conversation. While equally witty and entertaining, they are also good listeners and know when to offer a sympathetic ear to others.

WATER

Water signs: Cancer, Scorpio, Pisces

Water signs are in touch with their emotions, and are both empathetic and nurturing to others. Always ready to offer help, they will step up when they are needed. Water signs are imaginative and can be quiet thinkers.

EARTH

Earth signs: Capricorn, Taurus, Virgo

Earth signs are all about the details. While they are practical and grounded, they look to the future and start building for it way ahead of time. Earth signs are down-to-earth people and are often called the "gardeners of the zodiac", in part due to the care and attention they pay their family and friends.

The fifth element

Some Western sources believe in a fifth element known as the *quinta essentia* – or simply, "spirit". This element is frequently overlooked because it describes the soul or spiritual being of someone and stands apart from the other four elements. While some astrological applications take the fifth element into account when analyzing signs, it is not depicted in the horoscope.

Different astrological traditions

Over the centuries, different cultures around the world have developed their own astrological traditions and systems. It's fascinating to see how these differ and how they all came about.

WESTERN

In the West, the most commonly used astrological system is derived from the ancient form of astrology based on the 12 signs of the zodiac. This system spans popular culture in its basic form of sun sign horoscopes focusing on human behavior and motivation, and is led by the 12 constellations attached to the 12 sun signs.

MAYAN

Mayan astrology is based on an ancient and complex calendar known as the Tzolk'in, which consists of 20 day signs and 13 galactic numbers. The 260-day calendar is often used to suggest future events and identify different human characteristics. Instead of elements, the Mayan astrological system uses directions – north, east, south, west – which each carry a different set of meanings and a direction is assigned to each of the 20 day signs.

VEDIC

Vedic - or jyotish - astrology is derived from ancient Indian traditions and is one of the oldest and most-practiced forms of astrology in the East. While the vedic and Western zodiac follow pretty much the same 12 signs, the dates are different - for example, Aries runs from 13 April-14 May, while Taurus sits between 15 May-14 June (as opposed to 21 March-20 April for Aries and 21 April-21 May for Taurus in the Western calendar). This is because it is based on the fixed, observable positions of the related constellations, whereas Western astrology takes into account the shifting of the Earth on its axis over millennia and is instead based on the changeable position of the sun.

CHINESE

This system is based on the lunar cycles and the power of five elements - wood, fire, earth, metal and water. Drawing from ancient Chinese philosophy, and the concept of yin and yang, each year is associated with an animal as well as an element.

Different astrological techniques

There are many different astrological practices, but the ones outlined below are some of the most widely used across the world.

MODERN ASTROLOGY

Also referred to as "psychological astrology", this is the most popular type of astrology in the West and is the technique that will be the focus of this book. It is a practice with many layers, but in simple terms, modern astrology looks at the position of the planets in relation to your birth chart – which is a snapshot of the planets and stars on the day you were born – and uses the information to understand your personality, characteristics and behaviors.

Alan Leo was a respected British astrologer who revived the practice in the late 1800s and early 1900s, following its fall from favor at the end of the 1600s. Leo – who used his sun sign as a pseudonym – is widely referred to as the "father of modern astrology", thanks to the way he helped to move it away from fortune-telling and encouraged people to use it to explore behavior and personality through a psychological lens.

HORARY

The Horary astrology technique is rooted in ancient Hellenistic traditions and seeks to answer a question by creating a horoscope for the moment the question is asked. The astrologer will generally receive a simple "yes" or "no" answer to the question being posed.

MUNDANE

Mundane astrology studies the effect of the planets on groups of people, places and countries. This branch of astrology focuses on significant events throughout history and looks to understand it through the creation of a birth chart for that moment in time. A horoscope can then be created for that event to explain how people might react to or cope with such an event.

ELECTIVE

Elective astrology looks at the optimal time for an event to occur, based on the position of the planets. An astrologer might advise you to get married at a time when Venus – the planet of love and harmony – is aligned with the planet's position on your own birth chart, for example.

RELATIONSHIP

This branch of astrology looks at how compatible two individuals are likely to be in love. An astrologer will study the birth charts of the two individuals to see how well they will get along. There are two ways of doing this. The first is synastry, which compares the two birth charts side by side; and the second is composite, which involves calculating the midpoints of the planets on each person's birth chart to create a new chart for the pairing, which is then interpreted afresh.

TRADITIONAL

Until the twentieth century and the introduction of modern astrology, most branches of the practice were considered "traditional". This form is all about prediction and only uses the seven "planets" we can see with the naked eye to do so, namely the Sun, Moon, Mercury, Venus, Mars, Jupiter and Saturn.

LOCATIONAL

Locational astrology looks at a birth chart to determine where the bearer should exist or spend time. According to the position of certain planets in relation to the subject's own, they can advise where they should live or go on holiday. If someone wanted to know where they were likely to have the most successful holiday, for example, an astrologer might look at the position of Venus (representing enjoyment) and Jupiter (long-distance travel) in order to deduce the ideal location. This is also known as "astro-mapping".

MEDICAL

Medical astrology is all about the health of a person, whereby an astrologer uses an individual's birth chart to discover the cause of any health issues they may have. The health problem, cures and area or areas of the body in which it occurs all correspond to specific planetary positions.

Science fiction?

Modern astrology is more popular than ever, with younger generations increasingly adopting the practice in an attempt to understand their own lives. And they hold it in high esteem: a National Science Foundation poll conducted in recent years found that more than half of millennials believe astrology to be a science.

What astrology can do for you

Astrology does not predict your future or describe your personality in certain terms; instead it describes the potential for particular characteristics or events to come to light. Astrology can help you know what you are capable of as a human being, and when to take advantage of challenging or opportunistic times. Astrology does not negate your own free will – you are not controlled by the planets – but the planets do create certain atmospheres and conditions that you can learn to use to your advantage.

When you understand why you act in a certain way or acknowledge your fears and desires, you feel more at ease with yourself and your world. When you know yourself better you act with conscious awareness of what you're doing and why.

ASTROLOGY IS A LANGUAGE. IF YOU UNDERSTAND THIS LANGUAGE, THE SKY SPEAKS TO YOU.

DANE RUDHYAR

Part 2

MEET LEO

As the fifth sign of the zodiac, Leo loves basking in the spotlight. You adore being the center of attention in both your life and career, and are determined when you set your sights on what you want. You are a big-hearted, kind and generous soul, with the sunniest personality among all the sun signs. Leo has much to give – love, time, advice, money – and is a loyal friend until the end. This sign's need for control can sometimes be overbearing, but if Leo keeps this in check all will work out in the end. Over the following pages we'll take a more detailed look at what really makes you tick in all areas of life, from career to wealth, love and romance, relationships with friends and family, health and well-being, and compatible signs. We'll find out what the planets mean to you, as well as your strengths and challenges.

Factfile: Leo

DATES: 23 July–23 August

REPRESENTATION: Lion

SYMBOL:

CHARACTER TRAITS: Outgoing, popular, creative

BODY PART: Heart

ELEMENT: Fire

RULING PLANET: Sun

COLOR: Orange

BIRTHSTONE: Ruby (July), peridot (August)

ASSOCIATED CRYSTALS: Tiger's eye, rose quartz, garnet

CHAKRA: Crown

TRIVIA

+ Leo is the fifth sign of the zodiac, after Cancer and before Virgo. It is the second of the fire signs, the others being Aries and Sagittarius.

+ The word "Leo" means "lion" in Latin and this is the symbol for the constellation, widely believed in the Western world to represent the Nemean lion from the first of Hercules' labors from Greek mythology.

+ Leo is thought to be one of the earliest recorded constellations, with the Mesopotamians recognizing a "lion" constellation.

+ The Leo constellation is easy to locate because the "pointer" stars of the Big Dipper (also known as the Plough) point towards Leo. The pointer stars sit either side of the top of the "bowl" of the Big Dipper.

+ Leo's constellation can be found between Cancer to the west and Virgo to the east, and is visible in the northern hemisphere from the spring equinox until May.

+ The brightest star in the constellation is Algieba, which means "lion's mane" and three stars form Leo's haunches, the brightest of which is Denebola, which means "lion's tail".

The history of Leo

In Greek mythology, Leo is related to the myth of the 12 Labors of Hercules. The Greek goddess Hera induced a madness in Hercules that led him to kill his wife and children; Hercules was then assigned 12 difficult tasks as a penance. These included being faced with various violent situations involving ferocious beasts such as the Cretan bull, Lernaean hydra and Nemean lion.

The first labor saw him encounter a lion that had been terrorizing the inhabitants of the city of Nemea. The offspring of Zeus and Selene, the lion was rampaging through the streets, attacking those who lived within the city walls. The lion's skin was so tough that it could not be penetrated, and its claws and teeth were as strong as iron.

Hercules was tasked with slaying the lion and proceeded to shoot it with a succession of arrows; however, the arrows simply bounced off the lion's impenetrable skin. Hercules didn't give up and continued to fight the lion, losing a finger in the process.

Eventually, he managed to daze the lion by using his club to give it an almighty whack around the head. While the lion was seeing stars, Hercules saw his chance and strangled the beast until it breathed no more.

Zeus chose to bestow immortality upon the lion and sent it up into the sky where it became the constellation of Leo.

Leo:
what the planets tell us

One of the most important strands of astrology is what the planets can tell us when they are transitioning through your sun sign. You can find planetary transition predictions on various websites including this one: astrosage.com/transits. Note: as outer and therefore slower-moving planets, Uranus, Neptune and Pluto take hundreds of years to move through all 12 signs of the zodiac! Therefore what they can tell us is far broader and less personal.

The Sun: purpose – You long to be admired and firmly in the spotlight. Your drive to reach your goals could see you assuming a position of leadership.

The Moon: instinct – Your creative talents come to the fore, and you would do well to take these as far as you can; you are also keen to help nurture the talents of others.

Mercury: communication – You are able to command the attention of an audience with your clear and coherent voice and power to dazzle.

Venus: love – Your love of luxury shines through in your fashion choices; you make sure those close to you know how much you love them.

Mars: action – You are a born leader when it comes to sport and wherever your heart lies, you want to lead the team.

Jupiter: opportunity – Your self-assurance is perfect for the side of you that loves to perform, but make sure you keep any creeping arrogance in check.

Saturn: authority – Don't let nerves get you down when it's your turn to be in the spotlight. With the right focus you will find that all runs smoothly.

Uranus: change – Uranus represents sudden change and innovation, as well as the advancing of science and technology.

Neptune: imagination – As well as intuition, glamour and enchantment, Neptune moves us to ask ourselves important questions in the quest for another path.

Pluto: power – Pluto is about the bigger picture and not worrying about the small stuff. Due to its incredibly slow orbit, it can take between 12 and 30 years for Pluto to move through one sign – and a whopping 248 years to transition through the whole zodiac. This is why Pluto is known as "the generational planet", with whole generations finding Pluto on their birth chart.

2060 Chiron

Some branches of astrology also include 2060 Chiron, a minor planet in the outer solar system orbiting the sun between Saturn and Uranus. Discovered in 1977, it suggests that self-assurance will promote healing as you look to find independence from your situation.

Leo: personality traits and characteristics

The organizer of the zodiac, you are meticulous when it comes to keeping your affairs in order. You like to know where everything is in your home; you get a kick out of organizing and might even like a bit of color coding! Drawer dividers and storage containers are your vices. When you need to locate paperwork for a life/admin task you know exactly where to find it.

You're also a bit of a guru to others, keen to help them learn how to be super organized in their own lives. This is your enthusiastic and generous nature shining through. Try not to push people too hard, however – you think you know best, but they might like their cluttered home just the way it is.

This need for control can spill over into other areas and occasionally cause problems for you, so remember to take a step back regularly and think about whether you're taking things too far. Does your sock drawer really need ordering and color coding as a priority? The chances are that it can wait and there are more important things to focus on right now.

Leos are warm-hearted and kind individuals with a zest for life and a sunny disposition. You're fun-loving and say "yes" to almost anything, likely filling every moment of your free time with something meaningful. You have a good network of friends and there is always someone to call on when you're in the mood to socialize.

Leo:
strengths and challenges

STRENGTHS

✦ Sunny Leo is sociable, friendly and kind. You have the gift of gab and just know how to talk to people. You can put strangers at ease and are kind and charming to everyone you meet.

✦ You are a big-hearted soul, going out of your way to help others and extending this to those beyond your networking and social circles. You know when a cause is worth fighting for and you'll gladly step up in support.

✦ You are a sensational host when it comes to dinner parties – making sure your guests have everything they need and going above and beyond to add extra-special touches. As a friend you are fiercely loyal and protective and will do anything for those you love.

CHALLENGES

✦ Your love of organizing your own life and the lives of others can border on controlling behavior. Take a step back if situations grow too intense and think about how you might be making other people feel.

✦ While Leo loves the spotlight, sometimes your attention-seeking behavior can go too far. If you're the type to notice when you get like this, try to rein it in to avoid pushing people away.

✦ Ever dramatic, you might want to take the time to assess your reactions and think logically about the situation before flying off the handle. Think about the effect the melodrama can have on others' stress levels as well as your own.

Leo:
interests, likes and dislikes

INTERESTS

When it comes to hobbies, you are most at home with those that allow your creativity to shine. You like activities that leave you feeling productive and with something to show for your hard work – think gardening, creative DIY, sewing, knitting and crochet.

Dancing and ice-skating could also be on the agenda, along with gymnastics and martial arts such as taekwondo and tai chi – graceful disciplines that also allow room for thought and strength training.

LIKES

You love the spotlight. Being the center of attention just feels natural to you and you sometimes just can't imagine things any other way. It's important to learn to share the spotlight with others, however, especially close family members and friends.

You are a sociable creature and would far rather spend a night out with pals than home on the sofa with your cat. A "yes" person, you can find your diary bursting with parties, drinks, get-togethers, hobbies and activities. Remember to breathe and take a break from it all so you don't burn out.

DISLIKES

You are not a fan of awkward silences and fill any quiet moments with conversation and chatter. Don't be afraid to pause for thought and enjoy a break from the noise.

As someone who likes to be in control, when you lose it you can sometimes lash out. Try taking some time out to think things through or write down and collect your thoughts, and you'll get back to grips with things in no time.

Leo:
communication style

You're the one who strikes up conversations with strangers at bus stops. Your fire sign shines through in your warm and generous personality, you make friends easily and have a way with people that puts them at ease. Your sunny disposition precedes you. You're the friend who gets invited along everywhere, your pals safe in the knowledge you will get on with almost anyone, your easy-going nature and willingness to chat are key components of your social repertoire.

You know how to work the room at a party or networking event, with something to say to fill every awkward pause and the ability to put a positive spin on anything to deliver uplifting conversation.

You are not just chatty and friendly, you have a great sense of humor too. People tend to find you hilarious and everyone wants to sit next to you in the pub or at a dinner party. You can light up a room with no problem and brighten the mood with ease.

Your moral compass always points in the direction it should and you are not afraid to speak up when you feel something is unjust. You're a loyal lion who fights for your friends and will defend them to the end.

This extends to wider issues, your lion heart beating for all those in need, as you campaign for the rights of others too.

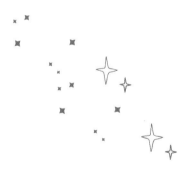

Leo: compatibility with other signs

Remember this is not hard and fast – the zodiac moves in mysterious ways and just because your sign might appear incompatible with that of someone you are close to doesn't mean a friendship or more is off the table. As always, the zodiac is just a guide.

Aries – These two fire signs bring serious energy and fun to the relationship, but are also able to tap into each other's emotional side.

Taurus – While both incredibly loyal and dependable, Leo and Taurus are also very stubborn, which can lead to a deadlock situation if you're not careful.

Gemini – Gemini loves the way Leo keeps them entertained, and Leo loves the way Gemini endlessly pays them compliments.

Cancer – These two signs are quite different in personality, but both share a similar flair for creative pursuits and will bond over their shared love of family.

Leo – Double Leo means fighting for the spotlight, but also a couple that are fiercely loyal to one another and share the same values.

Virgo – While quite different from one another, an intense energy in the bedroom can keep things moving.

Libra – Best friends and a very romantic coupling; Leo and Libra also bring high drama, which in a double dose can be intense.

Scorpio – This partnership is tense. Scorpio is less than patient with flighty and fickle Leo, but they both bring great passion to the relationship.

Sagittarius – These two fire signs keep the fire burning. Leo brings the romance, while Sagittarius provides the adventure.

Capricorn – Leo's warm to Capricorn's cool can either make for great balance in a partnership, or create something lukewarm.

Aquarius – These two strong-willed signs can find themselves at a standstill when the other won't back down, but creativity from both sides makes for an interesting relationship.

Pisces – Both bring sensitivity and empathy to the partnership, really listen to each other and know how to please each other between the sheets.

Leo: relationships – friends and family

Leos have a lot of love to give and go out of their way to make those who they care about feel important. You are interested in other people and keen to understand them. You can sometimes forget that not everyone thinks the same way and it's important to acknowledge differences. Don't assume others will want to do things the way you do them; listen, be understanding and open-minded, and you will make friends for life.

You love to entertain friends in your home and are forever hosting dinner parties and get-togethers. You are a warm and charming host, generous with both your time and food and drink for your guests.

Controlling Leo can often want to steer the group when friends or family spend time together. Be careful not to be too overbearing and be ready to listen to other people's ideas. Your way is not always the right way.

As a parent you are great at encouraging your children's interests and helping them to fulfil their potential. You are loving and nurturing, keen to help grow your offspring's enthusiasm to give them a wide and varied array of hobbies. Be careful to keep your ego in check, however, and recognize your child's own interests rather than forcing your own on to them.

Leo:
love and sex

Leos are generous in relationships – with time, money, gifts and in the bedroom. Your controlling nature can be a bit much for your partner if you don't learn to rein it in, so do your best to keep this in check. Let them have some independence from you – everybody needs their space – and let them make their own decisions. This is hugely important for the health of the relationship.

You have a lot of love to give your partner and your sunny personality can rub off on them a great deal, making for a very positive partnership. However, you can be sensitive when it comes to love and are hurt easily. For this reason you might find you are slow to commit, taking your time to ensure you're making the best move.

Leos can be possessive over their partners and jealousy can be quick to rise to the surface. Be wary of your behavior when the green-eyed monster comes to visit – and remember jealousy can be a huge turn-off.

Instead, make time to talk to your partner and explain how you're feeling. Being transparent about how things affect you will help them to understand you and hopefully be more sensitive in the future.

Leo:
career and success

Leos like to take center stage when it comes to their work life and can find themselves in careers that involve commanding the attention of a great many individuals, and a degree of emotional involvement is common too. Perhaps you'll be most at home in the classroom, a court-room, as the head of a company, in an operating theatre or literally treading the boards on stage as an actor.

You are creative and have a natural flair for original ideas and innovation. You might channel that creativity into starting your own business or following a career that involves making and tending things with your hands, be that in textiles, with raw materials or plants, or perhaps interior design or illustration.

Other career paths you might take include those that involve luxury or glamour – perhaps in the fashion world or luxury goods market.

Your generous spirit comes to the fore at work too; you are often willing to give up your free time to help others up the ladder through mentoring and offering advice whenever people need it.

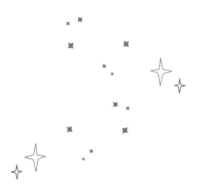

Leo:
money and prosperity

Leos have ambition in abundance, and this can often mean financial success is in the cards. Whatever your chosen field, you aim for the top, and if your area of expertise is a lucrative one it's likely you're doing okay when it comes to cash.

When it comes to holding on to that cash it can be a different story, however. Leos love the finer things in life and like to spend extravagantly on luxury rather than slumming it. This can mean that you spend money as fast as you earn it and barely have any left to save for a rainy day.

You also have an impulsive nature, which can be great when it comes to being a "yes" person and living your life to the fullest. However, when it comes to your love of luxury, it can mean you spend a lot on unimportant items without giving the matter much thought.

Add to this the fact that your incredibly generous nature extends to money and goods that you bestow on others – perhaps helping out a friend in need who has less than you do – and it's unlikely you have much to show for your regular pay check.

WITHOUT ASTROLOGY MAN TREADS, AS IT WERE, IN THE DIM TWILIGHT OF IGNORANCE.

LUKE DENNIS BROUGHTON

Leo:
health and well-being

Your busy life and constant need for the spotlight can mean you push yourself and don't always take the breaks you need to recuperate. It's important to switch off and practice some self-care when needed – even when you don't think it is. Incorporating a regular yoga class into your schedule can work wonders for your busy mind and body, giving you space to breathe. If you can fit it in, daily guided meditation for five or ten minutes will do you the world of good. It's important to look after your busy brain and ensure you don't burn out.

Regular outdoor exercise can also be a tonic for you and your creeping stress levels. Embrace outdoor pursuits that are good for the soul – get out in nature and go for a walk or a hike. You could even try some forest bathing – the Japanese have embraced this form of ecotherapy, which involves walking or immersing yourself in nature and consciously connecting with your surroundings. The benefits to your physical and mental health are manifold.

Wild or cold-water swimming is another way to use the benefits of nature to your advantage. Many fans of wild swimming claim to feel energized for the rest of the day following a dip, and the benefits of cold-water therapy are held in high esteem by many – look into the Wim Hof method if you want to know more.

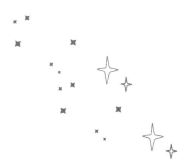

Part 3

YOUR HOROSCOPE AND YOU

This is where you start putting your knowledge into practice – it's time to build a birth chart. Over the following pages you'll learn how to do that and most importantly how to decode it. It might look complicated at first glance, but don't worry – all the elements and information you need to understand your chart are here in this chapter. We'll guide you through, step by step, and help you to make sense of it all. From your moon and rising signs, to the meanings hidden in the planets and houses, the mysteries of the night sky are about to be revealed.

Using astrology for divination and guidance

By mapping out a birth chart and discovering the position of the planets and zodiac signs in the sky and which particular astrological house they were occupying when you were born, you can gain a deeper insight into yourself. Armed with this knowledge you can learn more about who you are, your motivations and what makes you tick. You could also gain a greater picture of who you might become, what prospects lie ahead and how you can potentially work them to your advantage.

Whether you feel misunderstood or simply want some clarity, you might find solace in the sky. When big decisions loom, you might look to astrology for comfort and reassurance. While astrology does not spell out the answers, it will give you much to ruminate on and relate to. With the houses covering so many aspects of your life, and the planets and zodiac signs looking to your personality, there's a lot of coverage up there!

In the following pages you will learn how to cast your birth chart (this is much easier than it used to be, thanks to modern technology and the internet) and learn what all the segments and symbols mean; how to work out your moon and rising signs; and gain greater knowledge about the planets and houses, their influence on your life and how to interpret their meaning.

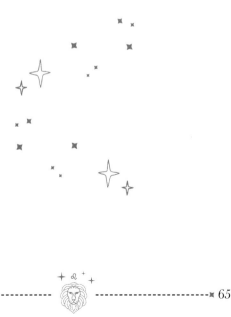

Dos and don'ts when interpreting the stars

DO

- ✦ Remember astrology is all about guidance

- ✦ Sleep on it before making any big decisions

- ✦ Seek a reading from an experienced astrologer if you are worried or need clarity on your reading

DON'T

- ✦ Take things too literally – these are interpretations, presented for you to find meaning in them in relation to your life

- ✦ Rush yourself – go at your own pace and all will become clear

- ✦ Obsess over your results – tomorrow is another day and things could change

**A CHILD IS BORN
ON THAT DAY AND AT
THAT HOUR WHEN
THE CELESTIAL RAYS
ARE IN MATHEMATICAL
HARMONY WITH THEIR
INDIVIDUAL KARMA.**

SRI YUKTESWAR

How to create your own birth chart

To create your birth chart you simply need to know the day on which you were born and the location. It is, however, vital that you know exactly what time you were born on that day. If you don't know, ask relatives, consult medical records or dig out your baby book – if you have one – because it is impossible to create an accurate birth chart without this information.

Sometimes referred to as a "natal chart", your birth chart is essentially a snapshot of the position of the planets and stars in the sky at the exact moment of your arrival on Earth. It's a wholly unique arrangement, never to be repeated, and can bring you so many valuable insights in your quest to better understand yourself.

Creating a birth chart used to be a painstaking process, but thanks to the power of the internet you can now be presented with yours in minutes. Try astro.com and opt for one of their free birth charts, from simple to complex; I say "simple" – even the simplest birth chart will look a bit indecipherable the first time you see one, but you'll soon get the hang of it.

TimePassages is a very user-friendly paid-for app where you can create a birth chart and read daily horoscopes based on your personal information and astrological transits – as well as compare your chart with a friend or partner's – should you want to delve a little deeper.

An example birth chart

Symbols

 ARIES

 TAURUS

 GEMINI

CANCER

 LEO

 VIRGO

 LIBRA

 SCORPIO

SAGITTARIUS

 CAPRICORN

AQUARIUS

 PISCES

PLANET SYMBOLS

 SUN

 MOON

 MERCURY

VENUS

MARS

JUPITER

 SATURN

 URANUS

NEPTUNE

 PLUTO

How to decipher your birth chart

It's a good idea to keep an open mind when reviewing your birth chart. Be flexible, be imaginative and be prepared to take on the challenges it presents. Explore the potential it offers and be open to suggestions you might not previously have expected.

We've talked about the signs of the zodiac already, and in the following pages we'll look at the planets and the houses. These are the most important elements of the birth chart.

You will find around the outer wheel the 12 signs of the zodiac, while the inner 12 segments that overlap these are the houses.

The line across the middle is the horizon, with "AC" for ascendant, or rising sign, and "DC" for descendant. Look to the vertical line and "MC" is for midheaven and "IC" for *imum coeli* (loosely translating as "bottom of the sky").

Now it's time to work out what it all means. Follow the instructions on the following pages to find out how.

THE PLANETS

Look at the planets one by one and where they are placed on the chart. The simplest way to explain these is that the planets tell you "what", the sign it is transitioning through tells you "how" and "why", and the house the planet appears in represents the area of life to which this is relevant. As the fifth sign of the zodiac, Leo rules the fifth house. This means that this particular house is associated with Leo energy. Looking at the example birth chart on page 70, the moon is transitioning through Taurus and the fifth house. From this we can take the moon to signify playfulness, and Taurus to represent grounding – perhaps a new love interest or a project that excites you – in the fifth house, which symbolizes creativity and pleasure.

PLANET CLUSTERS

Clusters of planets on the chart can also be revealing. The upper hemisphere of the chart represents your public life, while the lower hemisphere represents your private life. The west half represents freedom, while the east side represents fate. If there are more planets on one side than the other then this sways your reading.

LUNAR NODES

The lunar nodes are represented by the symbol ☊. These are the points at which the moon intercepts the sphere. Each astrology chart has a north and a south node, with the south node positioned directly opposite the north. Because the south node represents your past, who you have been, your instinctive behavior and your comfort zone, it doesn't tend to feature on birth charts, but is instead reserved for astrological readings later in life; the north node represents the opposite to the south node – where you should be heading in life, your aspirations and how you should challenge yourself to grow. The zodiac signs these two nodes fall into represent what these past and future characteristics should look like.

For example, on the birth chart on page 70, the north node falls into Aries, suggesting your future will see you standing out from the crowd and going with your gut when making big decisions.

**THE STARRY VAULT
OF HEAVEN IS IN TRUTH
THE OPEN BOOK OF
COSMIC PROJECTION.**

CARL JUNG

How to discover your moon sign

Your moon sign refers to the astrological sign the Moon was travelling through at the time of your birth. The Moon takes two-and-a-half days to travel through each sign, so around one month to complete a cycle of all the signs of the zodiac.

Understanding your moon sign is important because it speaks of your emotional nature – your fears, longings, obsessions and everything in between. It is often called the "soul of your identity" – the subconscious part of you that remains hidden and perhaps you don't even know that well. Learning more about your moon sign can help to unlock these hidden traits and help you to understand yourself better.

Some call your moon sign your "inner child", your closely guarded emotional centre. It can have a big impact on your mood and the way your emotions make their way to the surface.

You will know your sun sign, but it's important to calculate your moon sign too in order to gain the bigger picture. You will feel incomplete without it.

How to calculate
your moon sign

In the past, in order to determine your moon sign, you would have had to look up your time and date of birth in a planetary ephemeris – an extensive compendium of tables charting the Moon's position throughout the days, months and years. You can find your moon sign on your birth chart. For example, on the birth chart on page 70, the moon sign falls into Taurus, suggesting that you have a romantic nature and are attracted to creativity.

You do not need to create your birth chart to find out your moon sign, however. If you're after a quick answer you can use an online calculator such as lunarium.co.uk/calculators/moonsign. You will need to know the exact time of your birth, as a few minutes either way could push you to a different sign entirely.

Understanding your moon sign

Aries – You are an impatient soul, powering through life at a stressful pace. It can be hard to plan ahead when all you think about is what is happening right now.

Taurus – You take things slowly and cautiously, remaining calm and paying attention to every detail. You are tactile and feel the need to keep people close.

Gemini – You thrive on learning and taking in new information – whether through interactions with others or reading books.

Cancer – Security is very important to you and there is a deep-rooted urge to also keep those around you safe.

Leo – You love being showered with praise and seek it wherever you can. You are keen to nurture your own talents and help others find theirs too.

Virgo – You are practical when it comes to taking care of yourself and others. Well-being is important to you and self-care high up on your priorities.

Libra – You love company and are drawn to people with whom you can create easy friendships. Well-being is high up on your agenda, particularly when it involves calm and peace.

Scorpio – You wear your emotions on your sleeve and can find it hard to hold back. Try a fast-paced workout if you need to shake off these feelings.

Sagittarius – You like your own space and the freedom to do things your way. You prefer to travel solo and deal with your emotions on your own.

Capricorn – You are a fan of routine – structure works for you and helps you to navigate day-to-day life as well as retain a feeling of control.

Aquarius – You don't follow the crowd and always want to explore alternative options. A sense of community is important to you as you seek like-minded folk.

Pisces – Your emotions can often confuse you – as can how to deal with those of other people. Often a little time out is the ideal solution.

What is a rising sign?

Your rising sign, also known as your "ascendant", is the constellation that was rising on the eastern horizon at the time of your birth – and it's just as important as your sun sign!

As with your sun sign, there are 12 rising signs – from Aries to Pisces. While your sun sign reflects your personality, your rising sign reflects how you act.

For example, looking at the birth chart on page 70, if your sun sign is Leo you might have ambition in spades and a dramatic outlook, but with rising sign Scorpio you might act as quick-tempered and jealous. (See pages 18–23 for an overview of the zodiac signs and traits.)

Your rising sign is associated with the first house of your chart (see page 85 for more about the houses), so it's all about new beginnings and self-identity. Your sun sign represents a bigger picture of you, while your rising sign represents the surface of your personality, a first impression if you will.

How to calculate your rising sign

These days we only need to search online to discover our rising sign, but in the past astrologers had to put pen to paper to work it out.

Your rising sign is very specific to the time of day you were born and is essential for an accurate birth chart. The rising sign changes frequently, so this information is key. If you've ever encountered a pushy astrologer who insisted you give up this information – this is why! With all 12 signs of the Zodiac rising in a 24-hour period, each takes a 2-hour window, which can then be connected to the time of your birth. If you are born at sunrise, your sun and rising signs will be the same.

Twins born 15 minutes apart could well have different rising signs, meaning their birth charts – and therefore their personalities – could differ greatly from each other.

While you can gather all of this information from your birth chart, if you are after a swift answer you can calculate your rising sign here: astrosofa.com/ascendant.

How to calculate your descendant

Your descendant is the sign that was setting on the western horizon at the time of your birth, it lies directly opposite your ascendant, in the seventh house, which represents relationships (see page 85 for more about the houses).

The descendant describes your desires, who you get along with and who you are attracted to.

It represents external obstacles that challenge you on a daily basis and what you desire but cannot reach.

Your descendant sign is important in understanding your behavior in relationships and reflects experiences that can help you to understand issues in a partnership.

For example, in the birth chart on page 70, the descendant is Aquarius, suggesting you are warm and charming, and are attracted to interesting people, but need your independence in relationships.

To discover your descendant, look at your birth chart or use the same link you used to calculate your ascendant and scroll down for your full astrological profile: astrosofa.com/ascendant.

Understanding the planets in your birth chart

With each planet reflecting a part of our psyche, there is much to be gained from a deeper understanding of their meaning. The planets indicate how we react to people and situations, and outline our dreams and desires. Don't worry if some of the houses on your birth chart do not contain any planets – this is quite common! Each planet has a sign that it naturally rules – a sign that it is often found frequenting. Use the information below when interpreting your birth chart and refer to page 17 for your sun-sign-specific guidance on the planets.

The Sun is our ego, will and determination, orbiting all the signs of the zodiac in the space of a calendar year.

The Moon reflects the part of ourselves that remains hidden, our memories and inner emotions. It transitions into a new sign every two-and-a-half days.

Mercury is the planet of communication, news and travel. It can also reflect gossip and rumor.

Venus is the planet of love, romance, sensuality and beauty. It helps us understand our love for others, but also things.

Mars is the planet of energy, action and conflict.

Saturn is the planet of commitment and stability. It also represents the restrictions placed on us.

Jupiter stands for spiritual growth and helps us to understand any emotional issues we may have.

Neptune is often referred to as "poetry of the soul", reflecting our deep-rooted emotions and creativity.

Uranus represents rebellion and the fight for injustice – in both our personal lives and on a global scale.

Pluto looks to change and how it can allow us to grow and achieve our dreams. This is the planet that forces us to face our fears and conquer them.

Understanding the houses in your birth chart

While your birth chart is divided into 12 sections that represent the sun signs of the zodiac, there are another 12 sections overlapping these called the "houses". Each house represents a different aspect of your everyday life, from your career, to travel, to love and more. Every planet on your chart is located in both a sun sign and a house, and their positions are key to deciphering your birth chart and understanding more about your inner workings. The houses are complex and far-reaching; the pages that follow offer a brief insight to get you started, but if you want to probe deeper refer to Resources on page 125 to find out even more.

FIRST HOUSE: PERSONALITY

This is the house of the self; it represents you, the body you were born with and your temperament. This is the house that symbolizes birth and new beginnings, reflecting how we view our life, and how our earliest encounters have impacted us and shaped our world. When planets move into this house, our goals are manifested and fresh new ideas begin to form.

Planets in this house

Sun – Self-development
Moon – Deep feelings
Mercury – Connection
Venus – Beauty
Mars – Strength
Jupiter – Optimism
Saturn – Foresight
Uranus – Individuality
Neptune – Glamour
Pluto – Control

Zodiac signs in this house

Aries – Motivation
Taurus – Balance
Gemini – Communication
Cancer – Protection
Leo – Action
Virgo – Order
Libra – Grace
Scorpio – Self-defense
Sagittarius – Vision
Capricorn – Planning
Aquarius – Clarity
Pisces – Imagination

SECOND HOUSE: POSSESSIONS AND MONEY

This house is all about material possessions and personal finances. It tells you about your attitude towards money – do you love it or hate it? It also gives you an insight into your personal finances – perhaps they are a source of concern, perhaps you're good at saving for a rainy day, or you could be rather frivolous – and how you earn it and spend it. Beyond finances, anything to do with worth and value can be found in this house – what we consider valuable in life and how we value ourselves.

Planets in this house

Sun – Independence
Moon – Security
Mercury – Communication
Venus – Sensuality
Mars – Ambition
Jupiter – Confidence
Saturn – Frugality
Uranus – Change
Neptune – Charity
Pluto – Survival

Zodiac signs in this house

Aries – Self-motivation
Taurus – Accumulation
Gemini – Light-heartedness
Cancer – Possessiveness
Leo – Pride
Virgo – Thriftiness
Libra – Equality
Scorpio – Privacy
Sagittarius – Frivolity
Capricorn – Planning
Aquarius – Sharing
Pisces – Generosity

THIRD HOUSE: COMMUNICATION

This house is all about how you communicate with those around you. How you express yourself and build relationships with others in your life – whether friends, family, co-workers, neighbors or those in the wider community – is at play here and when planets move into this house you can receive information about your network of associations. This house also has a strong focus on the language element of communication and also the relationships you have with your siblings.

Planets in this house

Sun – Language

Moon – Education

Mercury – Connection

Venus – Harmony

Mars – Competition

Jupiter – Optimism

Saturn – Authority

Uranus – Single-
    mindedness

Neptune – Intuition

Pluto – Learning

Zodiac signs in this house

Aries – Rivalry

Taurus – Learning

Gemini – Connection

Cancer – Protection

Leo – Confidence

Virgo – Organization

Libra – Equality

Scorpio – Education

Sagittarius – Adventure

Capricorn – Planning

Aquarius – Rationality

Pisces – Imagination

FOURTH HOUSE: HOME AND FAMILY

This house reflects your home, the place you regard as your safe haven or where your family resides. It's about where you feel a sense of belonging, sanctuary and security. The family in this house refers not just to your relations, but the family you choose for yourself through friends, neighbors and those in your local community. This house reflects your relationship with the maternal figure(s) in your life and looks to the situations in which you feel loved and looked after.

Planets in this house

Sun – Identity
Moon – Privacy
Mercury – Conversation
Venus – Peace
Mars – Conflict
Jupiter – Travel
Saturn – Stability
Uranus – Independence
Neptune – Sanctuary
Pluto – Renovation

Zodiac signs in this house

Aries – Rivalry
Taurus – Security
Gemini – Loyalty
Cancer – Protection
Leo – Pride
Virgo – Duty
Libra – Diplomacy
Scorpio – Privacy
Sagittarius – Welcome
Capricorn – Organization
Aquarius – Community
Pisces – Music

FIFTH HOUSE: CREATIVITY AND PLEASURE

As well as creativity and pleasure, this house is also linked with leisure, romance and those tiny bringers of joy, children, as well as our legacy. This house is all about what makes you feel good and brings you joy – whether that's getting your teeth into a creative project, feeling the rush of a confidence boost thanks to a compliment or career success, or the excitement of a new partner or life milestone. Risk-taking also falls into this house, so gamblers and extreme-sports enthusiasts take note.

Planets in this house	**Zodiac signs in this house**
Sun – Attention	Aries – Action
Moon – Playfulness	Taurus – Grounding
Mercury – Impulsivity	Gemini – Romantic connection
Venus – Communication	Cancer – Caretaking
Mars – Competition	Leo – Joyfulness
Jupiter – Fertility	Virgo – Humility
Saturn – Strategy	Libra – Perfection
Uranus – Originality	Scorpio – Loyalty
Neptune – Artistry	Sagittarius – Travel
Pluto – Transformation	Capricorn – Caution
	Aquarius – Value
	Pisces – Romance

SIXTH HOUSE: HEALTH AND WELL-BEING

As well as health and well-being, this house reflects your daily routines, which include jobs around the house and perhaps the more mundane tasks that you don't tend to give a second thought. Here is where to look for help in streamlining your schedules.

While the body you are born with is reflected in the first house, it is in this house that the focus lands on the body you have created over the course of your lifetime. Self-care, work–life balance, as well as mental and physical health are all covered here.

Planets in this house

Sun – Purpose
Moon – Hospitality
Mercury – Networking
Venus – Unity
Mars – Movement
Jupiter – Satisfaction
Saturn – Construction
Uranus – Change
Neptune – Music
Pluto – Nutrition

Zodiac signs in this house

Aries – Productivity
Taurus – Calm
Gemini – Dexterity
Cancer – Caretaking
Leo – Authority
Virgo – Detail
Libra – Diplomacy
Scorpio – Activity
Sagittarius – Freedom
Capricorn – Attention
Aquarius – Equality
Pisces – Structure

SEVENTH HOUSE: RELATIONSHIPS

Directly across from the first house, the seventh house reflects your life-changing relationships – not just romantic partners, but all significant relationships in your life. This house will look at negative as well as positive aspects of those relationships – offering potential insight into any disagreements you might have experienced among your nearest and dearest.

Planets in this house

Sun – Individuality
Moon – Sensitivity
Mercury – Knowledge
Venus – Value
Mars – Assertiveness
Jupiter – Motivation
Saturn – Commitment
Uranus – Independence
Neptune – Longing
Pluto – Transformation

Zodiac signs in this house

Aries – Equality
Taurus – Stability
Gemini – Variety
Cancer – Sentimentality
Leo – Desire
Virgo – Grounding
Libra – Compromise
Scorpio – Intensity
Sagittarius – Company
Capricorn – Security
Aquarius – Supportiveness
Pisces – Selflessness

EIGHTH HOUSE: SEX, DEATH AND TRANSFORMATION

This is the house in which we experience the darker aspects of life – emotional crises, loss and devastation – as well as the rituals, trials and tribulations of our existence. This house also reflects our intense romantic partnerships and adaptability to the ever-changing nature of our lives. This house teaches us that we need to embrace compromise in order to move forward, accept change and learn to derive power and inner strength from loss.

Planets in this house

Sun – Exploration
Moon – Intuition
Mercury – Secrecy
Venus – Diplomacy
Mars – Decisiveness
Jupiter – Positivity
Saturn – Boundaries
Uranus – Clarity
Neptune – Connection
Pluto – Power

Zodiac signs in this house

Aries – Impulsivity
Taurus – Investment
Gemini – Exploration
Cancer – Privacy
Leo – Financial success
Virgo – Catastrophe
Libra – Equality
Scorpio – Lust
Sagittarius – Risk-taking
Capricorn – Independence
Aquarius – Rationality
Pisces – Excitement

NINTH HOUSE: PHILOSOPHY AND ADVENTURE

This house looks ahead towards what we don't yet know – what lies beyond the horizon. Travel and higher education are also represented here – and those with birth charts showing planets in their ninth house are often extremely inquisitive and adventurous when it comes to travel. This house represents uncharted territory and curiosity – searching for a greater understanding of ourselves – as well as faith and politics.

Planets in this house
Sun – Confidence
Moon – Wanderlust
Mercury – Language
Venus – Creativity
Mars – Fearlessness
Jupiter – Teaching
Saturn – Caution
Uranus – Enlightenment
Neptune – Spirituality
Pluto – Education

Zodiac signs in this house
Aries – Independence
Taurus – Patience
Gemini – Curiosity
Cancer – Connection
Leo – Luxury
Virgo – Preparedness
Libra – Equality
Scorpio – Education
Sagittarius – Limitless
Capricorn – Ambition
Aquarius – Community
Pisces – Escape

TENTH HOUSE: CAREER

As well as your professional aspirations, this house also takes in social status and popularity. If you have planets in the tenth house on your birth chart you are no doubt an ambitious person when it comes to work life – and you know how to socialize with gusto. If you are feeling somewhat in limbo, this house may help to guide you towards your calling. Career changes are afoot when planets transition into this house.

Planets in this house

Sun – Identity
Moon – Caring
Mercury – Networking
Venus – Diplomacy
Mars – Competition
Jupiter – Possibility
Saturn – Responsibility
Uranus – Independence
Neptune – Creativity
Pluto – Influence

Zodiac signs in this house

Aries – Self-starter
Taurus – Loyalty
Gemini – Variety
Cancer – Nurturing
Leo – Self-promotion
Virgo – Creativity
Libra – Diplomacy
Scorpio – Determination
Sagittarius – Achievement
Capricorn – Organization
Aquarius – Teamwork
Pisces – Compassion

ELEVENTH HOUSE: FRIENDSHIP

This is the house that recognizes our social circle, and is where we find our place in the networks and groups in our lives. Here we find friendship, teamwork and common goals represented, as well as our support network, acquaintances and the way in which we spend time with those in our lives. Our social and political values come to the fore in this house, as does our ability to work with others to improve situations.

Planets in this house

Sun – Community
Moon – Extroversion
Mercury – Networking
Venus – Charm
Mars – Competition
Jupiter – Broadmindedness
Saturn – Commitment
Uranus – Freedom
Neptune – Self-sacrifice
Pluto – Empowerment

Zodiac signs in this house

Aries – Energy
Taurus – Constancy
Gemini – Diversity
Cancer – Safety
Leo – Leadership
Virgo – Caring
Libra – Harmony
Scorpio – Force
Sagittarius – Initiative
Capricorn – Control
Aquarius – Equality
Pisces – Sympathy

TWELFTH HOUSE: SACRIFICE

Sometimes known as the house of the unconscious, the twelfth house is also referred to as "the darkness before the dawn" – sitting just below the horizon, finishing off the houses before the cycle begins again. The "unconscious" speaks of all things without physical form, such as dreams, emotions and secrets. Planets take on an otherworldly quality in this house and this is where your good deeds are recognized.

Planets in this house

Sun – Purpose
Moon – Compassion
Mercury – Imagination
Venus – Self-reflection
Mars – Courage
Jupiter – Generosity
Saturn – Dedication
Uranus – Freedom
Neptune – Charity
Pluto – Acceptance

Zodiac signs in this house

Aries – Initiative
Taurus – Relaxation
Gemini – Ambition
Cancer – Caring
Leo – Creativity
Virgo – Thoughtfulness
Libra – Balance
Scorpio – Intuition
Sagittarius – Escape
Capricorn – Structure
Aquarius – Recharge
Pisces – Boundaries

Part 4

ASTROLOGY FOR SELF-CARE

We all need a little self-care in our lives and astrology can help steer you towards practices most suited to your sun sign and characteristics. As a Leo, your mind is constantly abuzz with thoughts, ideas and strategies. Sometimes this can mean you lie awake at the end of a long day, your brain filled with noise and chatter. You might like your life fast-paced, but it's still important to slow down regularly and take in your surroundings so you don't miss anything. Many Leo people find their best self-care can be found in relaxing and mindful activities, such as yoga and meditation, in order to keep the mind and body happy, while others look to journaling to relieve any tension. What helps you to de-stress? The following pages offer some ideas to help you find the methods best suited to you.

How to use astrology to guide self-care practices

By aligning your self-care practices with your sun sign, you can really boost their healing power. It's worth doing the research to get the most out of your downtime and rest. When it comes to yoga there are poses that offer a greater benefit to one sign over another, according to your personality and behaviors; and you will find favor in the crystals that match your sun sign, allowing energy to flow more freely with those assigned to you.

The following pages contain self-care rituals and practices specific to you and your sign. From tarot to crystals, the celestial body and your chakras, and de-stressing techniques, as well as the types of exercise that could suit you best.

As a Leo, you are focused on so many things at once that your thoughts rarely have time to pause. Not only are you concerned about your own life, but you think a lot about others too. This can be exhausting. Make room for some self-care in your life, remember that sometimes you need looking after too and take some time out to relax and improve your sleep. You could try writing your thoughts and wishes in a journal or incorporating five to ten minutes of guided meditation into your day to banish any unhelpful thoughts.

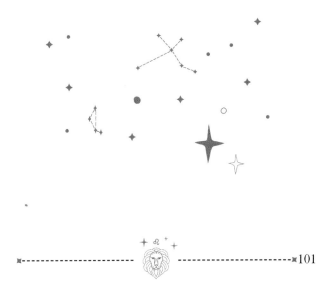

Dos and don'ts

DO

+ Go at your own pace; self-care is not a race

+ What feels right; not every suggestion will be the one for you

+ Allow the guidance to help you to change bad habits

DON'T

+ Push yourself too hard; if you have a minor injury but the guidance is to do some strenuous exercise, give it a miss until you're feeling better

+ Give up things you love just because they're not mentioned as specific to your sign

+ Take risks if something doesn't feel right – stay safe and comfortable

**WE ARE MERELY THE
STARS' TENNIS-BALLS,
STRUCK AND BANDIED
WHICH WAY PLEASE THEM.**

JOHN WEBSTER

Rituals to help Leo de-stress and unwind

You love nothing more than being out with friends somewhere loud and exciting. When it comes to getting your all-important rest, however, a more chilled-out activity before bed could really help you to relax into slumber.

A busy brain can be hard to quieten when there's been a lot going on during the day, so try heading to bed early for some restorative sleep and introduce a bedtime routine to really wind down. Spray lavender on your pillow and all around your bedroom, banish screens for at least an hour before bed and get comfortable with a good book or magazine.

If you need some help dropping off, investigate Calm, an app designed to help you de-stress and alleviate anxiety through guided meditation, sleep stories and soothing sounds. You'll likely find you don't reach the end of a sleep story before you are lulled into a deep slumber. Try the free version to see if it works for you before you sign up.

Writing in a journal before you go to bed can be a good step in a bedtime routine and help you banish unhelpful thoughts by writing them down before you go to sleep.

Try to scribble down three things you are grateful for before you go to sleep every night – these can be simple things that happened that day or bigger elements of your life. You'll find that the more you do this, the more positivity you bring into your life.

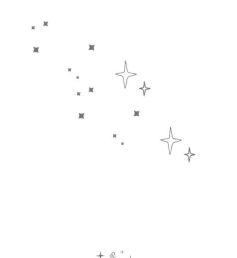

Yoga poses for Leo

The benefits of yoga are far-reaching, from increasing flexibility, improving muscle strength and tone, boosting energy, promoting circulation and restorative sleep, to bringing you a sense of zen and relaxation. The following yoga poses are ideal for you – and as a high-energy Leo you might also like to look into Bikram and flow styles of yoga.

Always make sure you warm up first and don't push your body. If you haven't tried yoga before, consider joining a class taught by an experienced yoga practitioner.

LION POSE

This stress-relieving pose brings strength to the lungs and throat, as well as stimulating the immune system.

Sit cross-legged on your mat with your palms face up, resting on your knees. Inhale and sit up straight, lengthening your spine. Imagine a thread attached to the crown of your head is gently pulling you upwards. Exhale and place your palms on the floor in front of you. Arch your spine, look up, open your mouth, stick your tongue out and roar like a lion!

HALF-CAMEL POSE

This pose opens up the chest while stretching the upper arms and shoulders.

Kneel on your mat, with your knees hip distance apart. Place your palms on your sacrum, with your fingers pointing down. Inhale and press your knees into the mat, lifting the crown of your head and lengthening your spine. Exhale and push your hips forward, squeeze your buttocks and thighs, and carefully reach your right hand down towards your right heel. If you cannot reach your heel, keep your hand on your sacrum. Inhale and reach up with your left hand, then, deepening your back bend, take your arm over to point behind you. Hold for a couple of breaths and release. Now perform the stretch on the other side.

STARGAZER POSE

This pose gives you a strengthening back bend.

Kneel on your mat with your hips positioned over your knees. Stretch your right leg out to the side with your foot on the floor. Push down with the outer edge of your foot. Extend both arms up and out to your sides, and tilt your body to bring your right hand to rest on your right leg, either on the thigh or below the knee. Tilt your torso to the left and place your left hand on the ground, slightly behind you. Keeping your right leg in position, hold here for a few breaths. Then move into child's pose, knees together with head down and arms stretched out in front, for a rest before performing the stretch on the other side.

BOUND ANGLE POSE

This pose opens the hips and chest while lengthening the spine.

Sit on your mat and bring the soles of your feet to rest against each other, allowing your knees to bend out to the sides. Move your hands to your feet and interlace your fingers around your toes. Take a deep breath in and push your hips down while reaching the crown of your head up to lengthen the spine. Relax your shoulders and let them drop down and back, pushing out your chest. Bring your knees as close to the floor as you can in order to open up the hips. Sitting tall, keep your spine long and your chest open. Breathe out and gently take your torso forward. Close your eyes and hold for a few breaths. Then have a rest before performing this pose again.

THERE IS NO BETTER
BOAT THAN A HOROSCOPE
TO HELP A MAN CROSS
OVER THE SEA OF LIFE.

VARAHA MIHIRA

Exercise for Leo

Leos love to be around people, so team sports suit you down to the ground. You're often likely to find yourself in the position of organizer or team captain, leading the pack to victory and potentially the after party. Both the exercise and camaraderie make you feel good, and you are keen to make time in your busy schedule for both playing and socializing with your teammates.

You might find that running and yoga are the types of activities that can be slotted into your lunch-break when you need time out from a hectic day. Set an alarm if you're prone to get so stuck into work that you tend to breeze past lunchtime and find the tension rising come the end of the day.

Body-conditioning martial arts such as taekwondo are also good for Leos to build strength, stamina and patience. Using concise punching and kicking techniques alongside mental strength training, this ancient martial art's history is rooted in self-defense, with mind and body participating in equal measure. Equally, tai chi can allow Leo's graceful and creative side to shine.

A LION IN LOVE WILL CONQUER THE WORLD.

THERRIE ROSENVALD

Crystals

Naturally occurring crystals contain piezoelectric and pyroelectric properties that cause them to vibrate. This, along with the fact that they are also conductors of heat and electricity, has led many to believe that they have the ability to transform your energy levels, help you find love and restore your health.

Crystals have been used in healing for thousands of years and evidence of this can be found in ancient texts. The vibrations are thought to help restore the body's natural healing mechanisms, as well as encouraging a sense of balance, calm and well-being. This type of practice is called "vibrational medicine".

People often select crystals according to their color as well as their properties, and their sun sign and birth date can come into play here too. Choosing crystals with your sun sign in mind can help to align you for a more successful experience. Bearing in mind the celestial body (see page 36) and matching crystals to the chakra related to your sun sign (see page 122) will also bring the most benefits.

Chakra	Location	Color	Emotional and physical associations
Root	Base of spine	Red	Feeling grounded, independent
Sacral	Just below navel	Orange	Acceptance, well-being, pleasure
Solar plexus	Base of ribcage	Yellow	Confidence, self-control, self-esteem
Heart	Centre of chest	Green	Love, joy, inner peace
Throat	Base of throat	Blue	Communication, self-expression
Third eye	Above and between brows	Indigo	Intuition, decision-making
Crown	Top of head	Violet	A feeling of connection, spirituality

CRYSTALS ACCORDING TO ZODIAC SIGN

Aries – Red jasper, carnelian, citrine

Taurus – Smoky quartz, amazonite, selenite

Gemini – Shungite, amazonite, tiger's eye

Cancer – Selenite, labradorite, red jasper

Leo – Tiger's eye, rose quartz, garnet

Virgo – Amazonite, amethyst, fluorite

Libra – Tiger's eye, amethyst, bloodstone

Scorpio – Pink tourmaline, amethyst, raindrop azurite

Sagittarius – Lepidolite, smoky quartz, shungite

Capricorn – Rose quartz, garnet, smoky quartz

Aquarius – Lepidolite, amethyst, tourmalinated quartz

Pisces – Clear quartz, carnelian, chrysocolla

CLEANSE YOUR CRYSTALS

Preparing your crystals before use is important in order to remove any negative or old energy. Rinse them under running water for a minute and leave to dry outside in the fresh air. Then submerge your crystals in salt water and leave out to air dry. Finally, leave your crystals to bathe in moonlight or sunlight for 12 hours. Now they are ready to use.

SELF-CARE WITH CRYSTALS

You might want to try using crystals to create a calming space in your home, or an area in which you want to nurture creativity. Follow these simple steps to shift energy and transform your safe space.

✦ **Choose a quiet space in your home – perhaps an area of your living room or bedroom. Make sure this is a place where you can have a few moments away from any noise or other people, it is comfortable and you will be able to relax.**

✦ **Allow air to flow through the space in order to rid it of any "dead energy". Then do some more physical dusting and clean it up, clearing away any dust or cobwebs, and decluttering so only a few things remain.**

✦ **Add some crystals to bring a calm energy to the space – quartz and amethyst work well for this, promoting healing, cleansing and harmony.**

✦ **Put the crystals in a place where they will catch the natural light, and make sure they each have some space and are not touching each other.**

Tarot

Tarot can be used for divination and anyone can do a reading – you don't need to visit a psychic or be one yourself to dabble with the deck. Either perform your reading yourself or ask a friend to do it and take it in turns. Tarot can offer insight and guidance by asking a question and interpreting cards pulled at random from the deck. Each of the 78 cards holds a unique meaning in relation to the question being asked.

The cards are made up of the major and minor arcana. The 22 major arcana cards feature some you might have heard of before, such as the Sun, the Moon, the Fool, Death and the Lovers. These represent karmic influences and themes in your life. If one of these appears in your reading, it often signifies the need to reflect on its life lessons. Each zodiac sign is ruled by a card from the major arcana. In the case of Leo, the card is Strength – a card that features a lion in most decks and represents strength of heart, mind and soul, as well as physical strength.

The minor arcana features 56 cards grouped into four suits of 14 each; ten of these are numbered, along with a Page, Knight, Queen and King. These cards represent situations, guide you to make choices and reflect your state of mind.

Tarot itself is interpreted in different ways, with some believing the answers come from spirits or angels, while others favoring the explanation of synchronicity where the cards drawn are meaningfully related. If this is something that interests you, you're best to research tarot in more detail to understand the meanings behind each card, but the following pages will get you started with a few tips on how to set yourself up. With a little guidance, you can unlock the symbolism and begin a journey of self-discovery.

CHOOSING A DECK

It is supposedly bad luck to buy your first tarot deck yourself and believed that it should be given as a gift. However, this is often disregarded as archaic superstition, so if you're not bothered by that then go ahead and buy a deck yourself! It's important you have a good relationship with the deck of cards you end up using, so make sure you like the illustrations they feature. There are hundreds of different decks available, so do some research and choose some you like the look of. If you feel lost amid the variety, go for the ever-popular Rider-Waite-Smith deck.

ENERGIZING AND CLEANSING YOUR CARDS

A new deck needs to be energized, so once you've taken your cards out of their shiny wrapping be sure to give them a thorough shuffle. The best way to do this is to fan out the cards on a table and swirl them around until you're satisfied they're well and truly mixed up. Don't be precious, you want some of the cards to be upside down in order to give reversals in your readings, so swirl, mix and swirl again.

When you haven't used your deck for a while, it's a good idea to give it a cleanse to banish any negative energy. There are several ways you can do this: shuffle the deck and knock on it three times; place the cards on a window ledge overnight where they will be bathed in moonlight; burn some dried sage and pass the deck though the smoke a few times.

SETTING THE SCENE

In the beginning, it's a good idea to choose a space to practice where you will have some peace and quiet, and can give the deck your full attention. Choose a space that is calm and uncluttered – you want it to have a positive energy, so you could select a few items to help create the perfect space.

SETTING YOUR INTENTION

During a reading, it's vital you keep the positive energy flowing around you. An easy way to do this is to bathe the room in bright, white light – this will banish negative energy and keep it at bay for the duration of your reading.

READING AND QUESTIONING

Beginners are best off starting with a three-card spread, such as past, present and future. Make sure you have your question in your mind as you shuffle the deck. Cards that fly out of the deck while shuffling are symbolic. Deal three cards, face up, in front of you – past, present and future.

The more detailed the question you ask, the more detail you will have returned in your answer. Try to avoid vague questions or those that could have a simple "yes" or "no" answer. Think of questions that are more likely to open up a conversation. As a Leo, you might want to ask detailed questions related to your love life or what you're likely to achieve in the future. Who are you hoping to meet? What are you working towards at the moment? Ask the cards how it will all pan out.

WE NEED NOT FEEL
ASHAMED OF FLIRTING
WITH THE ZODIAC. THE
ZODIAC IS WELL WORTH
FLIRTING WITH.

D. H. LAWRENCE

Chakras

If you're into yoga, you might be familiar with chakras, or you might like to learn more. Rooted in Hinduism but practiced by many outside the faith, chakras are considered to be life forces that circulate energy to certain parts of our body. When the stresses and strains of life cause these to become blocked, we can feel the impact and it helps to work to unblock them. The best way to do this is by promoting the flow of energy via meditation, chakra-specific yoga poses and breathing exercises.

There are seven main chakras – the root, sacral, solar plexus, heart, throat, third eye and crown – these are separate from the parts of the body associated with each sun sign and instead correspond to a person's characteristics.

SUN SIGNS AND CHAKRAS

Aries – solar plexus, located in the abdomen, a source
of self-belief and power

Taurus – heart chakra, the energy of which brings
empathic skills

Gemini – throat chakra, associated with communication
and creativity

Cancer – third eye chakra, located on the forehead and
believed to be the centre of the soul

Leo – crown chakra, representing thinking,
understanding and arriving at solutions easily

Virgo – throat chakra, signifying clear communication
and public speaking

Libra – heart chakra, the source of emotional healing
and building bonds with others

Scorpio – solar plexus chakra, which helps to battle
fears and control emotions

Sagittarius – sacral chakra, bringing optimism and
passion

Capricorn – root chakra, located at the base of the
spine, promoting good mental and physical health

Aquarius – root chakra, helping to stay grounded
and supportive

Pisces – sacral chakra, promoting sensuality, emotion
and creativity

Farewell

How are you feeling about the zodiac now? You've learned so much! It's likely you've had a few "aha" moments while reading this book, with familiar scenarios and characteristics floating off the page. Many of us long to be understood better and astrology can provide some comfort amid the complexities of modern life.

Hopefully you now feel armed with the knowledge and insight you need to embark on the next phase of your journey. It's time for you to draw your own conclusions about who you are and why you behave the way you do – and the stars can help. The mystery of the zodiac is vast, but it is there to be unraveled and if you're up for the challenge you will certainly reap the rewards.

Resources

BOOKS

Goodman, Linda *Sun Signs* (1999, Pan)

Parker, Derek and Parker, Julia *Parkers' Astrology* (2021, Dorling Kindersley)

Taylor, Carole *Using the Wisdom of the Stars in Your Everyday Life* (2018, Dorling Kindersley)

WEBSITES AND APPS

Astro.com – a vast free resource for beginners and experienced astrologers; start by drawing up your birth chart using this website and move on from there

Linda-goodman.com – a useful forum dedicated to the late astrologer, where people share their astrological experience

TimePassages – user-friendly paid-for astrology app where you can create a birth chart as well as read daily horoscopes and compare your chart with a friend or partner's

Co-Star – popular astrology app (basic version is free) with slick design; a useful tool with real-time readings gleaned from NASA data and a wealth of information and insight

**ASTROLOGY IS LIKE
A GAME OF CHESS WITH
AN INVISIBLE PARTNER.**

NOEL TYL

Check out the rest of the series...

Based on the symbolism of the wheel,
Red Wheel offers books and divination decks
from a variety of traditions. We aim to provide the
ideas, information, and innovative approaches to
help you develop your own spiritual path.

Please visit our website, www.redwheelweiser.com,
to learn more about our full range of titles.